MART

W9-CTR-131

Special Meditations
for Health, Wealth, Love,
and Expression

By

REVEREND JOSEPH MURPHY

D.D., D.R.S., Ph.D., LL.D.

DeVorss & Co., *Publishers*
P.O. Box 550
Marina del Rey, California 90291

TABLE OF CONTENTS

CONSCIOUSNESS OF HEALTH

How to Apply the Healing Principle

Prayer for Health

Wearing His Garment

The Quiet Mind

Mental Poise

The Peace of God

The Gift of God

Controlling My Emotions

Overcoming Fear

The Holy Temple

HOW TO APPLY
THE HEALING PRINCIPLE

 will restore health unto thee, and I will heal thee of thy wounds, saith the Lord." The God in me has limitless possibilities. I know that all things are possible with God. I believe this and accept it whole-heartedly now. I know that the God-Power in me makes darkness light and crooked things straight. I am now lifted up in consciousness by contemplating that God indwells me.

I speak the word now for the healing of mind, body and affairs; I know that this Principle within me responds to my faith and trust. "The Father doeth the works." I am now in touch with life, love, truth and beauty within me. I now align myself with the Infinite Principle of Love and Life within me. I know that harmony, health, and peace are now being expressed in ~~my body.~~ OUR LIVES.

As I live, move, and act in the assumption of my perfect health, it becomes actual. I now imagine and feel the reality of my perfect body. I am filled with a sense of peace and well-being. Thank you, Father.

PRAYER FOR HEALTH

Jesus said, "Thy faith hath made thee whole."

I positively believe in the Healing Power of God within me. My conscious and subconscious mind are in perfect agreement. I accept the statement of truth which I positively affirm. The words I speak are words of spirit and they are truth.

I now decree that the Healing Power of God is transforming my whole body, making me whole, pure, and perfect. I believe with a deep, inner certitude that my prayer of faith is being manifest now. I am guided by the Wisdom of God in all matters. The Love of God flows in transcendent beauty and loveliness into my mind and body, transforming, restoring, and energizing every atom of my being, I sense the peace that passeth understanding. God's Glory surrounds me, and I rest forever in the Everlasting Arms.

WEARING HIS GARMENT

I have found God in the sanctuary of my own soul. God is Life; that Life is my life. I know that God is not a body; He is shapeless, timeless and ageless; I see God in my mind's eye. Through understanding I see and look upon God in the same way that I see the answer to a mathematical problem.

I now rise to the awareness of peace, poise, and power. This feeling of joy, peace, and good-will within me is actually the Spirit of God moving within me; It is God in action; It is Almighty. There is no power in external things to hurt me; the only Power resides in my own mind and consciousness.

My body is the garment of God. The Living Spirit Almighty is within me; It is absolutely pure, holy, and perfect. I know that this Holy Spirit is God, and that this Spirit is now flowing through me, healing and making my body whole, pure, and perfect. I have complete power over my body and my world.

My thoughts of peace, power, and health have the Power of God to be realized within me now. "Blessed are the pure in heart: for they shall see God." I have seen and felt His Holy Presence; it is wonderful.

THE QUIET MIND

God dwells at the center of my being. God is Peace; this Peace enfolds me in Its Arms now. There is a deep feeling of security, vitality, and strength underlying this peace. This inner sense of peace, in which I now dwell, is the Silent Brooding Presence of God. The Love and the Light of God watch over me, as a loving mother watches over the sleeping child. Deep in my heart is the Holy Presence that is my peace, my strength, and my source of supply.

All fear has vanished. I see God in all people; I see God manifest in all things. I am an instrument of the Divine Presence. I now release this inner peace; it flows through my entire being, releasing and dissolving all problems; this is the peace that passeth understanding.

MENTAL POISE

"Whither shall I go from thy Spirit? or whither shall I flee from thy Presence? If I ascend up into heaven, thou art there: if I make my bed in hell, behold, thou art there. If I take the wings of the morning, and dwell in the uttermost parts of the sea: Even there shall thy hand lead me, and thy right hand shall hold me." I am now full of a Divine enthusiasm, because I am in the Presence of All Power, Wisdom, Majesty, and Love.

The light of God illumines my intellect; my mind is full of poise, balance, and equilibrium. There is a perfect mental adjustment to all things. I am at peace with my own thoughts. I rejoice in my work; it gives me joy and happiness. I draw continually upon my Divine Storehouse; for It is the only Presence and the only Power. My mind is God's mind; I am at peace.

THE PEACE OF GOD

All is peace and harmony in my world, for God in me is "The Lord of Peace." I am the consciousness of God in action; I am always at peace. My mind is poised, serene, and calm. In this atmosphere of peace and goodwill which surrounds me, I feel a deep abiding strength and freedom from all fear. I now sense and feel the love and beauty of His Holy Presence. Day by day I am more aware of God's Love; all that is false falls away. I see God personified in all people. I know that as I allow this inner peace to flow through my being, all problems are solved. I dwell in God; therefore, I rest in the eternal arms of peace. My life is the life of God. My peace is the deep, unchanging peace of God; "It is the peace of God, which passeth all understanding."

THE GIFT OF GOD

"A merry heart maketh a cheerful countenance." The spirit of the Almighty pervades every atom of my being, making me whole, joyous, and perfect. I know that all the functions of my body respond to this inner joy welling up within me. I am now stirring up the gift of God within me; I feel wonderful. The oil of joy and illumination anoint my intellect and become a lamp unto my feet.

I am now perfectly adjusted emotionally; there is a Divine equilibrium functioning in my mind, body, and affairs. I resolve from this moment forward to express peace and happiness to every person I meet. I know that my happiness and peace come from God; as I shed His light, love, and truth to others, I am also blessing and healing myself in countless ways. I radiate the sunshine of God's Love to all mankind. His Light shines through me and illuminates my path. I am resolved to express peace, joy, and happiness.

CONTROLLING MY EMOTIONS

When a negative thought of fear, jealousy, or resentment enters my mind, I supplant it with the thought of God. My thoughts are God's thoughts, and God's Power is with my thoughts of good. I know I have complete dominion over my thoughts and emotions. I am a channel of the Divine. I now redirect all my feelings and emotions along harmonious, constructive lines. "The sons of God shouted for joy." I now rejoice to accept the ideas of God, which are peace, harmony, and goodwill, and I delight to express them; this heals all discord within me. Only God's ideas enter my mind, bringing me harmony, health, and peace.

God is Love. Perfect Love casteth out fear, resentment, and all negative states. I now fall in love with truth. I wish for all men everything I wish for myself; I radiate love, peace, and goodwill to all. I am at peace.

OVERCOMING FEAR

There is no fear, as "perfect Love casteth out fear." Today I permit Love to keep me in perfect harmony and peace with all levels of my world. My thoughts are loving, kind, and harmonious. I sense my oneness with God, for "In him I live, move, and have my being."

I know that all my desires will be realized in perfect order. I trust the Divine Law within me to bring my ideals to pass. "The Father doeth the works." I am divine, spiritual, joyous, and absolutely fearless. I am now surrounded by the perfect peace of God; it is "The peace of God which passeth all understanding." I now place all my attention on the thing desired. I love this desire, and I give it my whole-hearted attention.

My spirit is lifted into the mood of confidence and peace; this is the spirit of God moving in me. It gives me a sense of peace, security, and rest. Truly, "perfect Love casteth out fear."

THE HOLY TEMPLE

"Those that be planted in the house of the LORD shall flourish in the courts of our God." I am still and at peace. My heart and my mind are motivated by the spirit of goodness, truth, and beauty. My thought is now on the Presence of God within me; this stills my mind.

I know that the way of creation is Spirit moving upon Itself. My True Self now moves in and on Itself, creating peace, harmony, and health in my body and affairs. I am Divine in my deeper self. I know I am a son of the living God; I create the way God creates by the self-contemplation of spirit. I know my body does not move of itself. It is acted upon by my thoughts and emotions.

I now say to my body, "Be still and quiet." I must obey. I understand this, and I know it is a Divine Law. I take my attention away from the physical world; I feast in the House of God within me. I meditate and feast upon harmony, health, and peace; these come forth from the God-Essence within; I am at peace. My body is a temple of the Living God. "God is in His Holy Temple; let all the earth keep silent before Him."

ACCEPT ABUNDANCE

God is the Eternal Now

The Way of Prayer

How To Realize the Abundant Life

The Prayer of Faith

The Abundant Life

Imagination, the Workshop of God

God's Will For Me

Abide in the Silence

To Be, To Do, and To Have

GOD IS THE ETERNAL NOW

(Using the Subconscious Mind)

 know that my good is this very moment. I believe in my heart that I can prophesy for myself harmony, health, peace, and joy. I enthrone the concept of peace, success, and prosperity in my mind now. I know and believe these thoughts (seeds) will grow and manifest themselves in my experience.

I am the gardener; as I sow, so shall I reap. I sow God-like thoughts (seeds); these wonderful seeds are peace, success, harmony, and goodwill. It is a wonderful harvest.

From this moment forward I am depositing in the Universal Bank (my subconscious mind) seeds or thoughts of peace, confidence, poise, and balance. I am drawing out the fruit of the wonderful seeds I am depositing. I believe and accept the fact that my desire is a seed deposited in the subconscious. I make it real by feeling the reality of it. I accept the reality of my desire in the same manner I accept the fact that the seed deposited in the ground will grow. I know it grows in the darkness; also, my desire or ideal grows in the darkness of my subconscious mind; in a little while, like the seed, it comes above the ground (becomes objectified) as a condition, circumstance, or event.

Infinite Intelligence governs and guides me in all ways. I meditate on whatsoever things are true, honest, just, lovely, and of good report. I think on these things, and God's Power is with my thoughts of good. I am at peace.

THE WAY OF PRAYER

"Thou shalt make thy way prosperous, and then thou shalt have good success." I now give a pattern of success and prosperity to the deeper mind within me, which is the law. This inner voice leads, guides, and governs all my activities. I am one with the abundance of God. I know and believe that there are new and better ways of conducting my business; Infinite Intelligence reveals the new ways to me.

I am growing in wisdom and understanding. My business is God's business. I am Divinely prospered in all ways. Divine Wisdom within me reveals the ways and means by which all my affairs are adjusted in the right way immediately.

The words of faith and conviction which I now speak open up all the necessary doors or avenues for my success and prosperity. I know that "The Lord (Law) will perfect that which concerneth me." My feet are kept in the perfect path, because I am a son of the living God.

HOW TO REALIZE THE ABUNDANT LIFE

I know that *to prosper* means to grow spiritually along all lines. God is prospering me now in mind, body, and affairs. God's ideas constantly unfold within me, bringing to me health, wealth, and perfect Divine expression.

I am inwardly thrilled as I feel the Life of God vitalizing every atom of my being. I know that God's Life is animating, sustaining, and strengthening me now. I am now expressing a perfect, radiant body full of vitality, energy, and power.

My business or profession is a Divine activity, and since it is God's business, it is successful and prosperous. I imagine and feel an inner wholeness functioning through my body, mind, and affairs. I give thanks and rejoice in the abundant life.

THE PRAYER OF FAITH

"The prayer of faith shall save the sick and God shall raise him up." I know that no matter what the negation of yesterday was, my prayer or affirmation of truth will rise triumphantly over it today. I steadfastly behold the joy of the answered prayer. I walk all day long in the Light.

Today is God's day; it is a glorious day for me, as it is full of peace, harmony, and joy. My faith in the good is written in my heart and felt in my inward parts. I am absolutely convinced that there is a Presence and a perfect Law which receives the impress of my desire now and which irresistibly attracts into my experience all the good things my heart desires. I now place all my reliance, faith, and trust in the Power and Presence of God within me; I am at peace.

I know I am a guest of the Infinite, and God is my Host. I hear the invitation of the Holy One saying, "Come unto me all ye that labor, and I will give you rest." I rest in God; all is well.

THE ABUNDANT LIFE

"Consider the Lilies of the field; they toil not, neither do they spin; yet Solomon in all his glory was not arrayed as one of these." I know that God is prospering me in all ways. I am now leading the abundant life because I believe in a God of abundance. I am supplied with everything that contributes to my beauty, well-being, progress, and peace. I am daily experiencing the fruits of the spirit of God within me; I accept my good now; I walk in the light that all good is mine. I am peaceful, poised, serene, and calm. I am one with the source of life; all my needs are met at every moment of time and every point of space. I now bring "all the empty vessels" to the Father within. The fullness of God is made manifest in all the departments of my life. "All that the Father hath is mine." I rejoice that this is so.

"Where there is no vision, the people perish." My vision is that I desire to know more of God and the way He works. My vision is for perfect health, harmony, and peace. My vision is the inner faith that Infinite Spirit leads and guides me now in all ways. I know and believe that the God-Power within me answers my prayer; this is a deep conviction within me.

I know that the mental picture to which I remain faithful will be developed in my subconscious mind and come forth on the screen of space.

I make it my daily practice to imagine for myself and others only that which is noble, wonderful, and God-like. I now imagine that I am doing the thing I long to do; I imagine that I now possess the things I long to possess; I imagine I am what I long to be. To make it real, I feel the reality of it; I know that it is so. Thank you, Father.

"God opens for me the windows of heaven, and pours me out a blessing."

God's will must be God-like; for that is the nature of God. God's will for me, therefore, is health, goodness, harmony, and abundance.

"If ye abide in me, and my words abide in you, ye shall ask for what ye will, and it shall be done unto you." I am now enlightened by the truth; each day I am growing in wisdom and understanding. I am a perfect channel for the works of God; I am free from all worry and confusion. Infinite intelligence within me is a lamp unto my feet. I know I am led to do the right thing; for it is God in action in all of my affairs.

The peace that passeth understanding fills my mind now. I believe and accept my ideal. I know it subsists in the Infinite. I give it form and expression by my complete mental acceptance. I feel the reality of the fulfilled desire. The peace of God fills my soul.

ABIDE IN THE SILENCE

Jesus said, "God is a Spirit: and they that worship him must worship him in spirit and in truth."

I know and realize that God is a spirit moving within me. I know that God is a feeling or deep conviction of harmony, health, and peace within me; it is the movement of my own heart. The spirit or feeling of confidence and faith which now possesses me is the spirit of God and the action of God on the waters of my mind; this is God; it is the creative Power within me.

I live, move, and have my being in the faith and confidence that goodness, truth, and beauty shall follow me all of the days of my life; this faith in God and all things good is omnipotent; it removes all barriers.

I now close the door of the senses; I withdraw all attention from the world. I turn within to the One, the Beautiful, and the Good; here, I dwell with my Father beyond time and space; here, I live, move, and dwell in the shadow of the Almighty. I am free from all fear, from the verdict of the world, and the appearance of things. I now feel His Presence which is the feeling of the answered prayer, or the presence of my good.

I become that which I contemplate. I now feel that I am what I want to be; this feeling or awareness is the action of God in me; it is the creative Power. I give thanks for the joy of the answered prayer and I rest in the silence that "It is done."

TO BE, TO DO, AND TO HAVE

At the center of my being is Peace; this is the peace of God. In this stillness I feel strength, guidance, and the love of His Holy Presence. I am Divinely active; I am expressing the fullness of God along all lines. I am a channel for the Divine, and I now release the imprisoned splendor that is within. I am Divinely guided to my true expression in life; I am compensated in a wonderful way. I see God in everything and personified in all men everywhere. I know as I permit this river of peace to flow through my being, all my problems are solved. All things I need to fully express myself on this plane are irresistibly attracted to me by the Universal Law of attraction. The way is revealed to me; I am full of joy and harmony.

LOVE, PERSONALITY,
HUMAN AND FAMILY RELATIONSHIPS

God's Broadcast

Spiritual Rebirth

Love Frees

The Secret Place

Overcoming Irritation

Prayer of Gratitude

How to Attract the Ideal Husband

How to Attract the Ideal Wife

Divine Freedom

Prayer For World Peace

GOD'S BROADCAST

ll ye are brethren, for one is your father."
I always bring harmony, peace, and joy
into every situation and into all of my
personal relationships. I know, believe, and claim
that the peace of God reigns supreme in the mind
and heart of everyone in my home and business.
No matter what the problem is, I always maintain
peace, poise, patience, and wisdom. I fully and
freely forgive everyone, regardless of what they
may have said or done. I cast all my burdens on
the God-self within; I go free; this is a marvelous
feeling. I know that blessings come to me as I
forgive.

I see the angel of God's Presence behind
every problem or difficult situation. I know the
solution is there and that everything is working
out in Divine order. I trust the God-Presence implicitly; it has the *know-how* of accomplishment.
The Absolute Order of Heaven and His Absolute
Wisdom are acting through me now and at all
times; I know that order is Heaven's first law.

My mind is now fixed joyously and expectantly on this perfect harmony. I know the result is the inevitable, perfect solution; my answer is God's answer; it is Divine; for it is the melody of God's broadcast.

SPIRITUAL REBIRTH

Today I am reborn spiritually! I completely detach myself from the old way of thinking and I bring Divine love, light, and truth definitely into my experience. I consciously feel love for everyone I meet. Mentally I say to everyone I contact, "I see the God in you and I know you see the God in me." I recognize the qualities of God in everyone. I practice this morning, noon, and night; it is a living part of me.

I am reborn spiritually now, because all day long I practice the Presence of God. No matter what I am doing, — whether I am walking along the street, shopping, or about my daily business, — whenever my thought wanders away from God or the Good, I bring it back to the contemplation of His Holy Presence. I feel noble, dignified, and God-like. I walk in a high mood, sensing my oneness with God. His peace fills my soul.

LOVE FREES

God is Love, and God is Life; this Life is one and indivisible. Life manifests Itself in and through all people; It is at the center of my own being.

I know that light dispels the darkness; so does the love of the good overcome all evil. My knowledge of the power of Love overcomes all negative conditions now. Love and hate cannot dwell together. I now turn the Light of God upon all fearful or anxious thoughts in my mind, and they flee away. The dawn (light of truth) appears and the shadows (fear and doubt) flee away.

I know Divine Love watches over me, guides me, and makes clear the path for me. I am expanding into the Divine. I am now expressing God in all my thoughts, words, and actions; the nature of God is Love. I know that "perfect Love casteth out fear."

THE SECRET PLACE

"He that dwelleth in the secret place of the most High shall abide under the shadow of the Almighty."

I dwell in the secret place of the most High; this is my own mind. All the thoughts entertained by me conform to harmony, peace, and goodwill. My mind is the dwelling place of happiness, joy, and a deep sense of security. All the thoughts that enter my mind contribute to my joy, peace, and general welfare. I live, move, and have my being in the atmosphere of good fellowship, love, and unity.

All the people that dwell in my mind are God's children. I am at peace in my mind with all the members of my household and all mankind. The same good I wish for myself, I wish for all men. I am living in the house of God now. I claim peace and happiness, for I know I dwell in the house of the Lord forever.

OVERCOMING IRRITATION

"He that is slow to wrath, *is* of great understanding: but *he that is* hasty of spirit exalteth folly." I am always poised, serene, and calm. The peace of God floods my mind and my whole being. I practice the Golden Rule and sincerely wish peace and goodwill to all men.

I know that the love of all things which are good penetrates my mind, casting out all fear. I am now living in the joyous expectancy of the best. My mind is free from all worry and doubt. My words of truth now dissolve every negative thought and emotion within me. I forgive everyone; I open the doorway of my heart to God's Presence. My whole being is flooded with the light and understanding from within.

The petty things of life no longer irritate me. When fear, worry, and doubt knock at my door, faith in goodness, truth, and beauty opens the door, and there is no one there. O, God, thou art my God, and there is none else.

PRAYER OF GRATITUDE

"O give thanks unto the Lord; call upon His name; make known His deeds among the people. Sing unto him, sing psalms unto him: talk ye of all his wondrous works. Glory ye in His holy name: let the heart of them rejoice that seek the Lord."

I give thanks sincerely and humbly for all the goodness, truth, and beauty which flow through me. I have a grateful, uplifted heart for all the good that has come to me in mind, body, and affairs. I radiate love and goodwill to all mankind. I lift them up in my thought and feeling. I always show my gratitude and give thanks for all my blessings. The grateful heart brings my mind and heart into intimate union with the creative Power of the Cosmos. My thankful and exalted state of mind leads me along the ways by which all good things come.

"Enter into his gates with thanksgiving, and into his courts with praise: Be thankful unto him, and bless his name."

HOW TO ATTRACT THE
IDEAL HUSBAND

I know that I am one with God now. In Him I live, move, and have my being. God is Life; this life is the life of all men and women. We are all sons and daughters of the one Father.

I know and believe there is a man waiting to love and cherish me. I know I can contribute to his happiness and peace. He loves my ideals, and I love his ideals. He does not want to make me over; neither do I want to make him over. There are mutual love, freedom, and respect.

There is one mind; I know him now in this mind. I unite now with the qualities and attributes that I admire and want expressed by my husband. I am one with them in my mind. We know and love each other already in Divine Mind. I see the God in him; he sees the God in me. Having met him *within,* I must meet him in the *without;* for this is the law of my own mind.

These words go forth and accomplish whereunto they are sent. I know it is now done, finished, and accomplished in God. Thank you, Father.

HOW TO ATTRACT THE
IDEAL WIFE

God is one and indivisible. In Him we live, move, and have our being. I know and believe that God indwells every person; I am one with God and with all people. I now attract the right woman who is in complete accord with me. This is a spiritual union, because it is the spirit of God functioning through the personality of someone with whom I blend perfectly. I know that I can give to this woman love, light, and truth. I know I can make this woman's life full, complete, and wonderful.

I now decree that she possesses the following qualities and attributes: she is spiritual, loyal, faithful, and true. She is harmonious, peaceful, and happy. We are irresistibly attracted to each other. Only that which belongs to love, truth, and wholeness can enter my experience. I accept my ideal companion now.

DIVINE FREEDOM

"If ye continue in my word, then are ye my disciples indeed: And ye shall know the truth, and the truth shall make you free." I know the truth, and the truth is that the realization of my desire would free me from all sense of bondage. I accept my freedom; I know it is already established in the Kingdom of God.

I know that all things in my world are projections of my inner attitudes. I am transforming my mind by dwelling on whatsoever things are true, lovely, noble, and God-like. I contemplate myself now as possessing all the good things of Life, such as peace, harmony, health, and happiness.

My contemplation rises to the point of acceptance; I accept the desires of my heart completely. God is the only Presence. I am expressing the fullness of God now. I am free! There is peace in my home, my heart, and in all my affairs.

PRAYER FOR WORLD PEACE

Peace begins with me. The peace of God fills my mind; the spirit of goodwill goes forth from me to all mankind. God is everywhere and fills the hearts of all men. In absolute truth all men are now spiritually perfect; they are expressing God's qualities and attributes. These qualities and attributes are Love, Light, Truth, and Beauty.

There are no separate nations. All men belong to the One Country—the One Nation which is God's Country. A country is a dwelling place; I dwell in the Secret Place of the Most High; I walk and talk with God—so do all men everywhere. There is only One Divine Family, and that is humanity.

There are no frontiers or barriers between nations, because God is One; God is indivisible. God cannot be divided against Himself. The love of God permeates the hearts of all men everywhere. His wisdom rules and guides the nation; He inspires our leaders and the leaders of all nations to do His will, and His will only. The peace of God which passeth all understanding fills my mind and the minds of all men throughout the cosmos. Thank you, Father, for Thy peace; it is done.

EXPRESSION

Predicting My Future

My Destiny

Impregnating the Subconscious Mind

The Balanced Mind

The Creative Word

The Scientific Prayer

The Divine Answer

Prayer For Your Business

Right Action

The Resurrection Of My Desire

Achieving My Goal

Business Problems

Principle in Business

How To Solve Your Problems

Steps To Success

The Triumph Of Prayer

PREDICTING MY FUTURE

HOU MADEST HIM to have dominion over the works of thy hands." I know that my faith in God determines my future. My faith in God means my faith in all things good. I unite myself now with true ideas and I know the future will be in the image and likeness of my habitual thinking. "As a man thinketh in his heart so is he." From this moment forward my thoughts are on: "Whatsoever things are true, whatsoever things are honest, whatsoever things are just, whatsoever things are lovely, and of good report;" day and night I meditate on these things, and I know these seeds (thoughts) which I habitually dwell upon will become a rich harvest for me. I am the captain of my own soul; I am the master of my fate; for my thought and feeling are my destiny.

MY DESTINY

I know that I mold, fashion, and create my own destiny. My faith in God is my destiny; this means an abiding faith in all things good. I live in the joyous expectancy of the best; only the best comes to me. I know the harvest I will reap in the future, because all my thoughts are God's thoughts, and God is with my thoughts of good. My thoughts are the seeds of goodness, truth, and beauty. I now place my thoughts of love, peace, joy, success, and goodwill in the garden of my mind. This is God's garden, and it will yield an abundant harvest. The glory and beauty of God will be expressed in my life. From this moment forward, I express life, love, and truth. I am radiantly happy and prosperous in all ways. Thank you, Father.

IMPREGNATING
THE SUBCONSCIOUS MIND

The first step in the mental acceptance of your idea, desire, or image is to relax, immobilize the attention, get still, and quiet. This quiet, relaxed, peaceful attitude of mind prevents extraneous matter and false ideas from interfering with the mental absorption of your ideal; furthermore, in the quiet, passive, receptive attitude of mind effort is reduced to a minimum. In this relaxed manner, affirm slowly and quietly several times a day the following:

"The perfection of God is now being expressed through me. The idea of health is now filling my subconscious mind. The image God has of me is a perfect image, and my subconscious mind recreates my body in perfect accordance to the perfect image held in the mind of God."

This is a simple, easy way of conveying the idea of perfect health to your subconscious mind.

THE BALANCED MIND

"Thou wilt keep him in perfect peace whose mind is stayed on thee, because he trusteth in thee." I know that the inner desires of my heart come from God within me. God wants me to be happy. The will of God for me is life, love, truth, and beauty. I mentally accept my good now, and I become a perfect channel for the Divine.

I come into His Presence singing; I enter into His courts with praise; I am joyful and happy; I am still and poised.

The Still Small Voice whispers in my ear, revealing to me my perfect answer. I am an expression of God. I am always in my true place, doing the thing I love to do. I refuse to accept the opinions of man as truth. I now turn within and I sense and feel the rhythm of the Divine. I hear the melody of God whispering its message of love to me.

My mind is God's mind, and I am always reflecting Divine wisdom and Divine intelligence. My brain symbolizes my capacity to think wisely and spiritually. God's ideas unfold within my mind with perfect sequence. I am always poised, balanced, serene, and calm, for I know that God will always reveal to me the perfect solution to all my needs.

THE CREATIVE WORD

"Be ye doers of the word, and not hearers only, deceiving your own selves." My creative word is my silent conviction that my prayer is answered. When I speak the word for healing, success, or prosperity, my word is spoken in the consciousness of Life and Power, knowing that it is done. My word has power, because it is one with Omnipotence. The words I speak are always constructive and creative. When I pray, my words are full of life, love, and feeling; this makes my affirmations, thoughts, and words creative. I know the greater my faith behind the word spoken, the more power it has. The words I use form a definite mold, which determines what form my thought is to take. Divine Intelligence operates through me now and reveals to me what I need to know. I have the answer now. I am at peace. God is Peace.

THE SCIENTIFIC PRAYER

"Before they call, I will answer; and while they are yet speaking, I will hear."

When I pray, I call on the Father, the Son, and the Holy Ghost; the Father is my own consciousness; the Son is my desire; the Holy Ghost is the feeling of being what I want to be.

I now take my attention away from the problem, whatever it may be. My mind and heart are open to the influx from on High.

I know the kingdom of God is within me. I sense, feel, understand, and know that my own life, my awareness of being, my own I Amness, is the Living Spirit Almighty. I now turn in recognition to this One Who Forever Is; the Light of God illumines my pathway; I am Divinely inspired and governed in all ways.

Now I begin to pray scientifically in order to bring my desire into manifestation by claiming and feeling myself to be and to have what I long to be and to have. I walk in the inner silent knowing of the soul, because I know my prayer is already answered, as I feel the reality of it in my heart. Thank you, Father; it is done!

THE DIVINE ANSWER

I know that the answer to my problem lies in the God-Self within me. I now get quiet, still, and relaxed. I am at peace. I know God speaks in peace and not in confusion. I am now in tune with the Infinite; I know and believe implicitly that Infinite Intelligence is revealing to me the perfect answer. I think about the solution to my problems. I now live in the mood I would have were my problem solved. I truly live in this abiding faith and trust which is the mood of the solution; this is the spirit of God moving within me. This Spirit is Omnipotent; It is manifesting Itself; my whole being rejoices in the solution; I am glad. I live in this feeling and give thanks.

I know that God has the answer. With God all things are possible. God is the Living Spirit Almighty within me; He is the source of all wisdom and illumination.

The indicator of the Presence of God within me is a sense of peace and poise. I now cease all sense of strain and struggle; I trust the God-Power implicitly. I know that all the Wisdom and Power I need to live a glorious and successful life are within me. I relax my entire body; my faith is in His Wisdom; I go free. I claim and feel the peace of God flooding my mind, heart, and whole being. I know the quiet mind gets its problems solved. I now turn the request over to the God-Presence, knowing It has an answer. I am at peace.

PRAYER FOR YOUR BUSINESS

I now dwell on the Omnipresence and Omni-action of God. I know that this Infinite Wisdom guides the planets on their course. I know this same Divine Intelligence governs and directs all my affairs. I claim and believe Divine understanding is mine at all times. I know that all my activities are controlled by this indwelling Presence. All my motives are God-like and true. God's wisdom, truth, and beauty are being expressed by me at all times. The All-Knowing One within me knows what to do, and how to do it. My business or profession is completely controlled, governed, and directed by the love of God. Divine guidance is mine. I know God's answer, for my mind is at peace. I rest in the Everlasting Arms.

RIGHT ACTION

I radiate goodwill to all mankind in thought, word, and deed. I know the peace and goodwill that I radiate to every man comes back to me a thousand fold. Whatever I need to know comes to me from the God-Self within me. Infinite Intelligence is operating through me, revealing to me what I need to know. God in me knows only the answer. The perfect answer is made known to me now. Infinite Intelligence and Divine Wisdom make all decisions through me, and there is only right action and right expression taking place in my life. Every night I wrap myself in the Mantle of God's Love and fall asleep knowing Divine Guidance is mine. When the dawn comes, I am filled with peace. I go forth into the new day full of faith, confidence, and trust. Thank you, Father.

THE RESURRECTION OF MY DESIRE

My desire for health, harmony, peace, abundance, and security is the voice of God speaking to me. I definitely choose to be happy and successful. I am guided in all ways. I open my mind and heart to the influx of the Holy Spirit; I am at peace. I draw successful and happy people into my experience. I recognize only the Presence and Power of God within me.

The Light of God shines through me and from me into everything about me. The emanation of God's Love flows from me; It is a healing radiance unto everyone who comes into my presence.

I now assume the feeling of being what I want to be. I know that the way to resurrect my desire is to remain faithful to my ideal, knowing that an Almighty Power is working in my behalf. I live in this mood of faith and confidence; I give thanks that it is done; for it is established in God, and all is well.

ACHIEVING MY GOAL

"In all thy ways acknowledge Him, and He will make plain thy path." My knowledge of God and the way He works is growing by leaps and bounds. I control and direct all my emotions along peaceful, constructive channels. Divine Love fills all my thoughts, words, and actions. My mind is at peace; I am at peace with all men. I am always relaxed and at ease. I know that I am here to express God fully in all ways. I believe implicitly in the guidance of the Holy Spirit within. This Infinite Intelligence within me now reveals to me the perfect plan of expression; I move toward it confidently and joyously. The goal and the objective that I have in my mind are good and very good. I have definitely planted in my mind the way of fulfillment. The Almighty Power now moves in my behalf; He is a Light on my path.

BUSINESS PROBLEMS

I know and believe my business is God's business; God is my partner in all my affairs; to me this means His light, love, truth, and inspiration fill my mind and heart in all ways. I solve all of my problems by placing my complete trust in the Divine Power within me. I know that this Presence sustains everything. I now rest in security and peace. This day I am surrounded by perfect understanding; there is a Divine solution to all my problems. I definitely understand everyone; I am understood. I know that all my business relationships are in accord with the Divine Law of Harmony. I know that God indwells all of my customers and clients. I work harmoniously with others to the end that happiness, prosperity, and peace reign supreme.

PRINCIPLE IN BUSINESS

My business is God's business. I am always about my Father's business, which is to radiate Life, Love, and Truth to all mankind. I am expressing myself fully now; I am giving of my talents in a wonderful way. I am Divinely compensated.

God is prospering my business, profession, or activity in a wonderful way. I claim that all those in my organization are spiritual links in its growth, welfare, and prosperity; I know this, believe it, and rejoice that it is so. All those connected with me are Divinely prospered and illumined by the Light.

The Light that lighteth every man that cometh into the world leads and guides me in all ways. All my decisions are controlled by Divine Wisdom. Infinite Intelligence reveals better ways in which I can serve humanity. I rest in the Lord forever.

HOW TO SOLVE YOUR PROBLEMS

"What things soever you desire, when you pray, believe that ye receive them, and ye shall have them." I know that a problem has its solution within it in the form of a desire. The realization of my desire is good and very good. I know and believe that the Creative Power within me has the absolute Power to bring forth that which I deeply desire. The Principle which gave me the desire is the Principle which gives it birth. There is absolutely no argument in my mind about this.

I now ride the white horse which is the spirit of God moving upon the waters of my mind. I take my attention away from the problem and dwell upon the reality of the fulfilled desire. I am using the Law now. I assume the feeling that my prayer is answered. I make it real by feeling the reality of it. In Him I live, move, and have my being; I live in this feeling and give thanks.

STEPS TO SUCCESS

"Wist ye not that I be about my Father's business." I know that my business, profession, or activity is God's business. God's business is always basically successful. I am growing in wisdom and understanding every day. I know, believe, and accept the fact that God's law of abundance is always working for me, through me, and all around me.

My business or profession is full of right action and right expression. The ideas, money, merchandise, and contacts that I need are mine now and at all times. All these things are irresistibly attracted to me by the law of universal attraction. God is the life of my business; I am Divinely guided and inspired in all ways. Every day I am presented with wonderful opportunities to grow, expand, and progress. I am building up goodwill. I am a great success, because I do business with others, as I would have them do it with me.

I now let go of everything; I enter into the realization of peace, harmony, and joy. God is all, over all, through all, and all in all. I lead the triumphant life, because I know that Divine Love guides, directs, sustains, and heals me. The Immaculate Presence of God is at the very center of my being; it is made manifest now in every atom of my body. There can be no delay, impediment, or obstructions to the realization of my heart's desire. The Almighty Power of God is now moving in my behalf. "None shall stay its hand, and say unto it, 'What doest thou?'" I know what I want; my desire is clear-cut and definite. I accept it completely in my mind. I remain faithful to the end. I have entered into the silent inner knowing that my prayer is answered, and my mind is at peace.